NATIONAL GEOGRAPHIC

The World Solar Challenge

Pam Rushby

Contents

Introduction

Imagine a car race where no gas is needed. The World Solar Challenge is a race in which cars travel almost 2,000 miles and never have to have their tanks filled up with gas. This is a race for very special cars. These cars are powered by the sun.

▼ This American team built a solar car to race in the World Solar Challenge.

Solar Cars

The World Solar Challenge is the best-known race for **solar-powered** cars. Teams from countries all over the world, including the United States, Germany, Japan, and Australia, take part. Some teams are made up of students. Each team designs, builds, and races its own car.

If you stand at the side of the road when the cars go past, you'll see that solar cars don't look like other cars. Solar cars are close to the ground. They are **streamlined**, or shaped to move through the air quickly. They have dark **solar panels** on their bodies. These panels provide the power for the cars.

▲ This car, designed
by Australian high school
students, races down the
road.

The high school ▶
team rests at the
end of the day.

Power From the Sun

Sunlight is a source of energy. The dark panels on solar cars **convert**, or change, sunlight into electricity to power the cars' motors. Solar cars don't need much electricity to make them run. They use about the same amount of electricity as a toaster uses when it toasts a slice of bread.

◄ Members of the team from Taiwan clean the panels on their solar car.

Solar panels also help power other things. Perhaps you have a solar-powered calculator. Maybe you have seen houses that run on solar power. These houses have solar panels on their roofs. Sunlight hits the solar panels, and energy from the sun is converted into electricity.

The World Solar Challenge

The World Solar Challenge was first held in 1987. Drivers race 1,862 miles across Australia. Team members drive their solar cars from Darwin in the north to Adelaide in the south. They travel through some of the hottest parts of Australia.

The World Solar Challenge is held over ten days. The race starts at 8 a.m. in Darwin. The teams travel as far as they can until 5 p.m. Then they must stop to camp for the night. The race continues the next morning.

◀ The cars go through Kakadu National Park on the first day of the race.

START
Darwin

AUSTRALIA

•Adelaide
FINISH

- - - - - Race route

0 mi.   1,000
0 km   1,000

▲ This map of Australia shows the route taken by cars
in the World Solar Challenge.

The 2003 World Solar Challenge

Twenty-two teams from many countries entered the 2003 World Solar Challenge. The winning team crossed the finish line in four days. Other cars took ten days to finish the race. Some cars didn't finish at all!

Every race, people hope for good weather. Before the start of the 2003 World Solar Challenge, the weather was cloudy. Everyone was worried. Rain would slow down the solar cars. Luckily, the clouds cleared and the sun came out.

Did You Know?

Solar car racing is called a brain sport. This is because the teams use their brain power. They need to figure out ways to make their cars run faster and farther on solar power alone.

▼ The green car from Japan lines up to start the race.

And the Winner Is...

It's a record! Nuna II crossed the finish line on the fourth day. This car was built and raced by a team of 12 students from the Netherlands. Their time was more than an hour faster than the **previous** record.

▼ The crowd in Adelaide cheers the winning car, Nuna II.

The Suitcase Man

Detlef Schmitz from Germany has entered seven World Solar Challenge races. He is called "the suitcase man" because his car can be taken apart and packed in a bag. In 2003 Detlef and his car made it across the finish line for the first time. He arrived in Adelaide on the tenth day.

◄ When the weather warms up, Detlef takes the covers off his car and packs them away.

Solar Panel Problems

Students from Mannum High School entered a car named Christine in the race. Mannum High is a tiny school in a small Australian town. The team had problems with Christine's solar panels during the race, but they didn't give up. When the team finally arrived in Adelaide on the ninth day, half the town of Mannum was there to cheer.

▼ The Mannum High School car was missing many solar panels by the time it crossed the finish line.

The Next World Solar Challenge

Teams are already working on their cars for the next World Solar Challenge. Team members are inventing ways to make their cars go farther and faster. But they're doing much more than building racing cars. They're discovering new and better ways we can use energy from the sun as a source of power.

▼ Team members discuss new ideas to improve their car.

Glossary

convert   to change something into a different type or kind

previous   earlier

solar panel   a sheet of cells that change sunlight into electricity

solar-powered   powered by the sun

streamlined   having a shape that can move easily through air or water